DISENFRANCHISED

DISENFRANCHISED

What You Need to Know **Before Buying a Franchise** So You Don't Get Screwed

KARA CHMIELEWSKI

To reach the author: kara@novemcorp.com

ISBN: 978-1-962133-01-2

ACKNOWLEDGEMENTS

Owning and running a business is both very rewarding and very hard. Thank you to my husband, Steve, for being there from beginning to end supporting me in my endeavors in every way.

Thank you to my fellow franchisees, I'll never forget your help and kindness.

Ethics is knowing the difference between what you have a right to do and what is right to do. –Potter Stewart

You just can't beat the person who never gives up. –Babe Ruth

TABLE OF CONTENTS

INTRODUCTION

Many franchising books will advise you on how to go about "traditional due diligence" to assess a franchise. Generally, all this advice is important and must be performed, but traditional due diligence will not give you the full picture of the franchise system you are evaluating. It will give you the on-paper and best-case scenario view of the franchise, which—although very important—is not the whole story and, in some cases, not even close to the real story.

Think of the traditional due diligence process as similar to the hiring process. A candidate submits a résumé. On paper, the candidate may look great, get an in-person interview based on their résumé, and even perform wonderfully at the interview. However, when actually starting to work, this candidate may be woefully unfit for the role for reasons that were not apparent in the hiring process. You may have seen this before; I know I have.

Similarly, in a traditional due diligence process, potential franchisees read the "résumé" or franchise disclosure document (FDD) to learn about the franchise system. Then they meet with the franchisor, others in the corporate office, and "approved" franchisees in the system to find out more. In this process, the franchisor (as if a job candidate) tries to sell you on their franchise. It may not feel that way at the time; it may feel like you, as a potential franchisee, are the one being interviewed. You must focus on selling yourself instead of learning all that you can about the franchise system. And while many franchisors do vet their franchisees very carefully, the franchisor is also absolutely trying to sell you a franchise. If the franchisor meets with you in person, they have likely already approved you as a franchisee, but will almost always insinuate they are still sizing you up.

The big difference in this analogy is that an ill-fitting employee can easily be fired, but you cannot fire a franchisor once you own a franchise location. You cannot just walk away from it but must continue to abide by the franchise agreement you signed. The process of getting out of it can be horrendous and costly, so it is of the utmost importance to obtain a full, accurate view of a franchise system and franchisor **before** you buy it.

While I advise traditional due diligence, which includes reading other franchise books, working with a franchise attorney, etc., to learn a lot about the process, I also advise you to complete the steps outlined in this book to uncover a more accurate "warts-and-all" picture of your potential business. Knowing that most franchise agreements are, at a minimum, a **ten-year term,** you don't want to rush into this process or take it lightly. I have seen people quickly realize they bought into a franchise system that doesn't meet advertised goals and expectations and who end up having to endure franchise ownership with unkept promises, lack of support, and generally bad franchisor leadership. There is not enough franchisor accountability or oversight once a franchisee has bought into the system. A franchisor who lacks a plan for overall top-line growth or has little regard for maintaining expenses to protect franchisee profit can make franchisees' lives very difficult. Franchisors may choose to offload products and offer discounts to customers, which is unsustainable for franchisees. While these tactics may increase revenue for the franchisor in the short term, they likely do not help to grow the brand or increase the value of the franchise locations in any way. Additionally, the long-term effects of such a strategy may be detrimental to both the franchisees and the franchisor and, in the worst of cases, render franchises worthless.

A good franchisor will plan for top-line growth through new product innovations and marketing plans for the brand. When evaluating a franchise system, it's important to hear about the growth plan from franchise leadership; what products and services are coming in the future as well as about the systems in place to support franchisees to grow the overall brand. Some badly managed and led brands may instead focus more on milking their franchisees than having a "rising tide raises all boats" strategy through brand marketing and cost savings programs. Franchisors may frown upon franchisees discussing ways to optimize their specific locations. They may even subtly threaten those who continue to meet in an attempt to divide and conquer, or pit franchisees against each other to keep the franchisor power-over-franchisee arrangement intact.

Of course, these tactics are never found in an FDD or through franchisor-approved discovery meetings. Sometimes, franchisees are forbidden to share negative information through NDAs (non-disclosure agreements). Franchisees can be reluctant to share negative information as another franchisee may potentially wish to buy the location and seek to continue the ruse, creating a closed loop of only good information sharing.

Your own due diligence will ferret out the real story. No business deal is going to be perfect, but getting a realistic version of the truth is critical for decision-making. However good or bad your decision is to buy a franchise, it will affect every day of your life during your franchise ownership, so take your time and learn the truth about the franchise **before** you buy it.

This book is intended to augment your research and offer information to potential franchisees as a bit of a cautionary tale. Many franchisees have had great experiences, but many have not, so I hope this book helps to round out your due diligence process.

CHAPTER 1

A FRANCHISEE'S STORY

When I purchased my franchise, I had been a customer of the business for 10 years. I loved my experiences when I visited various locations of this brand. I wholeheartedly supported their mission, which was to provide a space to experience health and wellness services, learn about at-home solutions, and generally receive self-care. I purchased gift certificates from this brand for my bridesmaids as gifts. Knowing how much I loved the services, I thought it would be a considerate gift to allow them to take some time for themselves after helping with my wedding plans. Before buying my franchise location, other franchise locations I had visited were very helpful to me and provided just the perfect respite from my busy corporate role.

It was then that I was at a crossroads in my career, wanting autonomy and control of my work and seeking a new opportunity to grow my career. I had worked as an independent consultant in the corporate space and found marketing my services as a one-person business to be daunting; I thought franchising would be a great way to "partner" with a brand I loved and be a small business owner. I had saved money from my corporate career and independent consulting and knew I would work hard to grow my business through this brand and considered owning multiple locations. That was the dream.

In performing all the normal due diligence—including hiring an attorney to review the documents, meeting with many current franchisees, and talking with multiple people who worked at the corporate office—one would expect to learn enough about a franchise to make an educated decision. That may be the case for many franchise systems but I suggest more is involved to thoroughly review a franchise opportunity.

As one investigates potential franchise businesses, I believe there is a tendency to become blinded by the idea of it all. You may not see some red flags in the excitement of the sales process. The franchisee–franchisor arrangement is one of power and must be fully understood by potential franchisees. An unethical or inept franchisor and a franchise lacking the proper systems can truly make one's life a living hell.

You may think you are too smart to fall for a bad business deal. Maybe you are, but in this book, you'll find crucial information that you just might need to ensure you are buying a solid, reputable business and that you are the right person to own that particular franchise. Take your time. There is no rush. It is a huge commitment and the decision is weighty.

In this book, I outline four key areas to explore to confirm that you are making a good investment. Each franchise system is different regarding products and services, leadership, length of time in business, geographic location, etc., so tailor your diligence to get answers to your questions for each facet. This will be invaluable as you move through this process. Even if you decide owning a franchise is not right for you, this book offers other options to think about as potential next steps in your career.

Much of what is out there about owning a franchise puts a positive spin on it because many businesses profit from franchises. However, this book encourages great caution when evaluating a franchise. As a franchisee, you will be the one to vet whether it's the right business and a good fit for you. I know many who own franchises and feel they made a great decision, financially and otherwise. A good, pragmatic approach to evaluating a potential franchise is important, and the knowledge shared here can help fortify your decision.

I implore you to investigate any franchise you are thinking of investing in. Some well-intentioned people start to franchise their business before really understanding what it means, and then when gullible franchisees buy them, it creates a mess for all. I want to save you from being chained to a franchise system unworthy of your diligent effort and hard-earned money.

If you have purchased a franchise that is not a good fit or one in which the financial model does not work as described, the contract can feel like a prison sentence. Some refer to it as "indentured servitude" or "buying yourself a low-paying job." This can also put a massive strain on your mental health. A franchisor who does not understand what franchisees are going through and instead chooses to alienate or criticize them creates an extremely painful environment for franchisees. Family and friends get tired of hearing about the problems you are experiencing or may feel that your misery just confirms your bad decision of buying a franchise in the first place and so may feel a bit smug about your predicament. Many simply don't understand or assume you are just not up to the task of running a business. All of this adds to the burden you must endure daily.

In many cases, a franchisee may need their franchisor's help to find a buyer when they are ready to sell their location, but if there is no process, obligation, or desire on the franchisor's part to help a franchisee in this regard, it can leave a franchisee without good options to exit the system. Some franchisors wait for the franchisee to become so desperate that they will sell the business to the franchisor for pennies on the dollar, leaving the franchisee with nothing to show for their years of work, or even facing bankruptcy and lawsuits. Franchisors are likely to have much lower overhead than the franchisee since the necessary products and supplies may already belong to the franchisor.

But even at lower overhead costs, a franchise system with a failing business model is not going to survive. One franchisor, having blamed franchisees for years of stagnant revenue, soon discovered that their franchise wasn't growing because they were not leading the company for advancement or didn't care to create a profitable business model for their brand. They had been clinging to revenue received from franchisees by nickel and diming the franchisees instead of focusing on growing the bottom line for all involved. The franchisor simply may not care about the success of its franchisees. For a franchisee, this is a very painful and lonely situation to be in with no easy way out.

This experience is far from unique. Google "franchisee horror stories" to quickly confirm this truth.

CHAPTER 2

YOUR STORY

If you're reading this book, you are likely considering buying a franchise business. I want to help you make a more informed decision. I hope this book will better prepare you to consider potential problems as you conduct your due diligence.

You are probably very motivated, work hard, and seek an opportunity to make money while growing a franchise system in a mutually beneficial manner. I do think those franchise systems exist, but not all franchisors want to help franchisees grow their franchises. Some focus on growing revenue through questionable practices—another thing not found in franchise documents or even by an attorney reviewing your paperwork as much of it is boilerplate and produced by the franchisor. Just as when you take a new job at a company with a new boss, things can quickly become unclear if you have hitched your wagon to an unethical or incompetent franchise system. Unlike a job, however, you cannot just give two weeks' notice or tell the boss to "take this job and shove it." You "bought the farm" and now must figure out how to sell it or close it with the franchisor's approval and pay off all the debts incurred.

You need to know what you are buying and who you are going into business with. Owning and running a franchise business will control your work and life for years to come. This isn't an exaggeration. The franchise is your business but you are required to follow many rules and the franchisor and franchise system hold power and control over you and the success of your asset.

I want to help make sure you "look under the hood" of your considered franchise to be certain you have uncovered all you can to make a more informed decision. I believe there is a tendency to keep franchisees in the dark during the sales process; with any sales pitch, the franchisor is putting their best foot forward. Many franchise systems strategize to make a potential franchisee feel like they have been "chosen" to buy a franchise, when the franchisor's only requirement is that you have the money. I know many truly are in the franchise business to grow their overall brands and have every desire for their franchisees to succeed so I'm not disparaging **all** franchisors, but more than just a few franchisors don't care to help grow individual franchisee's profits. Some simply don't know how to plan for others' growth and focus on themselves. It is unfortunate for ethical and capable franchisors that there are bad elements in the industry, but you must be aware of them to avoid them.

In the next part of this book, I identify four specific areas that necessitate a deep dive before you consider buying a franchise. First, it is critical to understand the overall franchisor–franchisee relationship to see whether you are a good fit to even be a franchisee. A franchisee's business outcome largely depends on the franchisor. Yes, you would likely have some autonomy in running your franchise location, but a franchisor has an inherent "power over" franchisees that must be understood. If you determine that you'd like to continue to explore franchising, there are three further areas to cover:

- Deciding whether the franchise is worth your investment
- Investigating the leadership of the franchise system
- Understanding the path to getting out of the franchise

I invite you to assess each franchise opportunity logically and objectively. Do not get into the mindset that you can make the system better or think you will earn more money than all the other franchisees. It is natural to get excited over the potential, be all gung-ho as you learn about each opportunity, and feel like you are getting closer to the dream of business ownership. But some franchisors play into this and will say you'll likely profit more than other franchisees just to increase the likelihood that you will buy one.

As a small business mentor, I have run across this scenario many times and cringed. If a franchisor is bad-mouthing other franchisees before you've even purchased one, it is a red flag. A franchise is a system of processes and procedures under a brand name. You may be the hardest worker in the world with great plans to grow your franchise, but you will also be bound to the franchisor in ways that will stunt your growth if the system does not value the growth of its franchisees.

Chapter 3

VITAL CONSIDERATIONS

The serious consideration of a franchise purchase requires insight into your role as a potential franchisee and details about the franchise system you are considering. Each franchise system operates differently; don't put all franchise opportunities in the same bucket. Consider each franchise as you work through this book to make sure you are evaluating it on its own merit. Franchise systems' longevity ranges from decades old to start-ups to those in decline. Some have saturated the market, others are unknown to customers. Examine the growth stage of the brand, type of business, leadership, and so on, as these are vital factors. Ask questions and don't feel that any are out of bounds. The franchisors **are** the franchise system and can answer anything you ask—and they should be forthcoming with information. If they are not, that is a red flag.

I can't emphasize enough how important it is to do this exploration **before** you commit a cent. Owning a franchise is very different from owning an independent business or being an employee. Owning an independent business gives you the freedom to make every decision yourself; you choose your business hours, procedures, systems, and more, and decide when it's time to close your business completely. Granted, there are other factors to consider in independent businesses, such as employees and landlords, but you have the autonomy to make decisions you can't as a franchisee. Employees of a company have the right to quit their job at will. Of course, your employer can also let you go, so there really isn't much security in the role, but you are not legally and financially tied to it if it's a bad fit for you.

However, it is not easy, quick, or cheap to quit being a franchisee. To separate from your franchise agreement often requires finding a franchisor-approved buyer to replace you or paying the franchisor to take over your franchise. If you find yourself owning a franchise that has many of the issues I identify in this book, each day can be extremely difficult. Again, I don't believe any franchise system is perfect; there are pros and cons in any business relationship, but going into it with your eyes wide open is important.

Here are some high-level pros and cons of owning a franchise:

PROS	CONS
Systems are already set up; a known brand requires less overall marketing	Paying the franchisor or vendors for these systems is generally non-negotiable
Training to learn the business and systems	Systems are defined by the franchisor; generally, you must comply with them all
Fewer start-up/growing pains	Hard to get out of it
Support for you	Must follow franchisor rules
Keeps brand image positive and growing	Attached to the brand even if its image deteriorates

To make an informed decision about franchising, you should be able to answer an emphatic YES to each of these questions:

1. Are you a good franchisee candidate?
2. Is the franchise worth your investment?
3. Do you want to be in business with this franchise's leadership?
4. Is there an acceptable path to exiting the franchise?

In the next chapter, we get started with the first question: Are **you** a good franchisee candidate? You've worked hard for the money to purchase or finance your dream of business ownership so let's ensure it will be a good decision for you.

Chapter 4

ARE YOU A GOOD FRANCHISEE CANDIDATE?

To answer this question, you need to understand the franchisor–franchisee relationship. The franchisor has control over you, as a franchisee, and your business, the franchise. The franchise agreement signed by both parties is where many high-level promises are made. However, it is quite one-sided as the franchisor holds a lot of power, even to the extent that they can make changes to the agreement that you must abide by. The franchise agreement exists to maintain brand consistency in all of its franchises by requiring adherence to the rules and regulations. But for some franchisors, this agreement has also been used as a tool to control franchisees in suspect ways.

Many people go into franchising believing they have bought themselves autonomy but this isn't always the case. It is important to know what you want and choose a franchise that aligns with it. Reflecting on your goals, management style, skills, finances, principles, and more can be beneficial in determining how the franchisee role might fit you, where you would most likely thrive, and more importantly, where you likely would struggle. Nothing will be perfect, but understanding yourself is helpful as you evaluate each particular franchise system. Then, learn all you can about each franchise system and what is required as a franchise owner to compare with your ideal work week to see if they align.

Remember that each franchise system brand operates differently and you must evaluate each opportunity individually. For example, a McDonald's franchise system has been in business for decades and has very specific, detailed processes to maintain the consistency of its well-known products. On the other hand, a tutoring or gym franchise may be much more liberal in outlining steps for product and service delivery, allowing you to tailor the service a bit more to your style. Each franchise system also offers different levels of support in various areas, and you will need to learn about the systems of each franchise. Remember not to lump all franchise systems into one bucket when deciding whether you are a good franchisee candidate. Consider all aspects of each franchise opportunity and determine if you could work with the set of rules and systems each franchise requires.

For example, I like to have control over the operation of my business but highly value the branding and training a franchise system can offer. A well-known and loved brand name brings customers right to you, and the training provided is helpful if you are not an expert on the products or services offered. It may be worth it to surrender some autonomy in advertising for the brand recognition that draws clients from opening day. Again, identify what is most important to you in a franchise business so you know it when you see it.

The structure of the franchisor–franchisee relationship is not a partnership. Many tasks, rules, and processes a franchisee commits to may include maintaining certain business hours, providing prescribed services and products in a specific manner, purchasing certain equipment from the franchisor, and subscription services, etc. You can be fined or otherwise penalized if you do not comply exactly with the rules of the franchise system; this is to maintain brand consistency and system support from the franchisor. In a perfect world, the agreement would protect franchisees and assure the brand image is maintained by **all** franchisees within the system supporting overall brand growth. It would also mean a franchisor creates and maintains a brand and establishes leadership to develop growth plans that keep customers flocking to the brand for years to come.

You can negotiate a bit as the franchisor writes the franchise agreement terms, but you may be beholden to your franchisor for obtaining products, marketing, training, systems, etc., requiring regular interaction with and payment to the franchisor and staff. There is a lot of leeway for the franchisor to adjust things over time, so it's important to understand that as a franchisee, first and foremost, you are a follower of their rules. Perhaps there is some flexibility as to what additional services you can offer or local promotions to run, but some franchisors run blanket promotions that may not be profitable for independent franchises and can significantly cut into profits. This practice can also make one wonder if it is an intentional strategy—to drive a franchisee into needing to "sell" their business back to the franchisor at a later time.

Franchisees are often forced to offer products or services purchased from the franchisor but then make little to no profit after paying overhead and staff. I know franchisees who asked a franchisor about these practices and there were negative repercussions for questioning the promotions. Much is beyond your control so establish limits of what you will and won't accept before buying a franchise. Each one has different requirements and systems. Examine them.

You are required to follow the franchise agreement and the franchisor generally has the right to modify things, as is expected when a business changes over time. In good situations, this creates growth and progress for both the franchisor and franchisee. In unhealthy environments, this can create growth for the franchisor but increase costs and reduce profit for franchisees. A franchisor might require upgrades in equipment or fixtures, new products, and so on that must be purchased from the franchisor, immediately increasing the franchisor's revenue but significantly impacting a franchisee's cash outlay, who waits a long time to see ROI (return on investment). For example, a gym franchisor may require franchisees to purchase upgraded equipment directly from the franchisor, as it is specifically branded for the franchise system. These updates may not be a manageable expense for franchisees but a franchisor can require it. Cutting into a franchisee's profit too often can effectively cause a franchise to become unprofitable.

It's your franchise, but it's not really **your** business and the franchisor plays a large role in the success or failure of your franchise. You don't make the rules but you still have to follow them even when they change and even if you don't like them. In the best franchise systems, the rules benefit all parties involved: The franchisor plans and leads the franchise system into huge growth and you're thrilled to have the leadership to help you to grow your location and there are plenty of profits for all. However, in the worst of franchise systems, you may feel broke, bullied, trapped, jerked around, and mentally exhausted.

In the next few chapters, we talk more about how to assess a specific franchise and its management, but it is important to first learn how you align (or don't) with the structure of a franchisor to see whether it is something to explore further. Many franchisees underestimated the franchisor's ability to negatively affect their business; they think they can make their location successful regardless of the franchisor, but that is not always possible. And as this relationship isn't something that you can just quit, understanding the dynamic and determining if you can thrive in this type of arrangement is vital. Considering all of the pros and cons of franchising and understanding your propensity for fitting the franchisee profile can reveal whether being a franchisee is for you. Traits generally considered to be very useful for franchisees include:

- General understanding of accounting and finance
- Hard-working and able to work as many hours as necessary
- Flexibility with time and tasks
- Results-driven
- Team player, even when disagreeing with strategy and programs
- Good leadership and management skills
- Ability to learn
- Working under pressure while multi-tasking

Each franchise opportunity offers different levels of support. For example, a franchise system may have a great company-wide inventory management system to help you organize inventory but you may be required to pay for such services monthly or annually as part of your franchise agreement.

Being a franchisee is a bit of a dance between following the franchisor's rules and systems and leading and managing your own location to profitability and career satisfaction. When sales and profits are good, even the worst of franchise systems can be tolerated. It's when things are not good that bad franchise systems are revealed and it can be very tough for a franchisee. Know your limits for tolerating such an arrangement so you can determine whether you should become a franchisee or when to remove yourself from the system by planning for your exit.

Are you a good franchisee candidate? Ask yourself:

- Can I follow rules even if I don't agree with them?
- Am I a self-starter who can lead others?
- Am I willing to do everything from sweeping the floors to firing staff and anything else necessary?
- Am I available to work on short notice?
- Do I have a general understanding of accounting and finance?
- Am I able to put in the long hours likely necessary in the early years of business ownership?
- Am I willing and able to learn new things?
- Am I capable of leading and managing?

- Am I comfortable working under pressure?
- Am I flexible with my time?
- Am I capable of asking for help in areas where I am not knowledgeable?
- Are my goals mostly aligned with the franchisor's and the other franchisees'?
- Can I adhere to the culture, procedures, time requirements, and so on, or will I be bumping against the norm?
- Would I have the moral support of friends and family?

CHAPTER 5

IS THE FRANCHISE WORTH YOUR INVESTMENT?

In this section, we will explore how to determine whether a specific franchise opportunity is worth your investment. Every franchise system is different so taking time to investigate is invaluable to learning all that you can before making a decision. Remember, you are buying access to a system and you want to ensure your success in your chosen franchise. In completing all of the "normal" due diligence, you will review the franchise's documents and meet with the corporate office who will tell you all the great things about buying one of their franchises.

Smart investors don't take anything at face value. It is time for your own reconnaissance to get to the truth, get others to tell you how it really is, and find out where the tough spots are. While owning a franchise is typically a long-term commitment and things will change over time, getting a good picture of how things are today and how they have transpired can help to assemble a complete picture.

You must find out how effective the systems and processes are to understand how your daily work life as a franchisee will be. Obviously, no business deal is perfect; there are positives and negatives in even the best franchise systems. The key here is to get a good fact-based understanding of what is behind the deal because it's unlikely you've been told all that you need to know to make an informed decision. The normal process for vetting a franchise is biased and everyone you have talked to so far is essentially working for—or at least sugar-coating—the franchisor and brand.

You must get answers to these key questions:

- Is this franchisor ready to have franchisees?
- What is the financial picture of both franchisor and franchisee?
- What is the time commitment required for this franchise?
- How is marketing handled and how much is needed/expected for your franchise?
- What areas of the business will you be responsible for and have control over?
- Is there a support system available besides the franchisor?

Let's consider each question one by one.

Is this franchisor ready to have franchisees?

Some franchisors are not set up properly to have successful franchisees because their "systems" are not set up to support franchisees as one would expect. I've learned through mentoring franchisees that this can be the case with franchise systems making promises to install certain systems but then not having them in place or not until a future time, creating additional expense for franchisees. The lure for a franchisor can be a strong one. Why *wouldn't* someone who has established a successful location think that having more locations could replicate their concept and duplicate their earnings on each new location? The franchisor may have the best intentions of wanting to share a "proven" concept with others—it can and does work for some—but when it doesn't work, the franchisees are the collateral damage. Some franchise systems have not taken the time and money to figure out what being a franchisor means before jumping in. And when this happens, it can be devastating to franchisees both personally and financially, especially if the franchisor chooses to milk their franchisees dry because of their own errors through a lack of systems and planning. Running even a single very successful location can cause a small business owner to believe that they can also be a successful franchisor. However, the skills required to run a location or two are not likely the skills needed to be a successful franchisor.

A brand franchisor must provide support, processes, and procedures to its franchisees, along with the rights to use the brand's name and likeness. Being on the wrong end of this can be hell. Cost structures for franchisees are generally higher than for a franchisor-owned location. Franchisors are looking to benefit financially and grow the brand by having franchisees, but these costs are passed on to the franchisees and often reduce profits for an independent franchisee-owned location, harming them more than a company-owned franchise location.

A franchisor must understand how to scale its operations for growth. In my experience, some franchisors believe they can figure it out as they grow, and some do. However, many don't have the skills to put together a plan that includes all of the processes, procedures, and systems required to support growth. You don't want to be a guinea pig for an inept franchisor-in-training.

For example, one franchisor promises to staff franchisees with properly certified staff (as required by law) before opening day, but it did not happen. A cobbled-together solution left the franchisee vulnerable to legal repercussions from day one. The franchisee was led to believe that part of what he was buying with the franchise fee was the franchisor's ability—through their own training program—to identify and recruit the staff required by law. Right up to opening day, the franchisee was told that the right staff would be provided but was not.

You may be thinking, *The franchisee should have demanded the requirement be met!* He did. But if he had closed while waiting for the franchisor to "fix" the problem, he would have put his other staff at financial risk. In addition, paying his rent was at risk and he would have lost the benefit of his personal marketing spend before opening—including all the appointments he had booked before opening. The franchisor didn't seem to care and knew they essentially "had him by the balls" and that he needed to "make the donuts." So, he kept the doors open while waiting for the franchisor to make good on their promise. Soon thereafter, he was visited and fined by for not having the required staff member on site. It put the franchisee at a disadvantage and confirmed that support was not going to be provided as promised. He began to feel like he'd made a poor decision. Of course, during sales negotiations, he was told that the franchisor would do everything necessary to support staffing the business as required by law. However, this was not outlined in the franchise agreement and is an example of how the normal due diligence process will not tell you all that you need to know. In hindsight, had he listened more when talking with existing franchisees during his due diligence, he would have known that this could happen. He was blinded by both his desire to be a franchisee of the brand and naive to the possibility of such a lack of support; he thought he would actually be provided the basic support required.

Verify that what they say they are providing they are, in fact, providing. To do this, you need to speak to franchisees and job shadow at other locations, make many phone calls, and ask probing questions; don't stop until you are satisfied. Find contacts in the franchise system, meet them for coffee, and listen carefully to how they answer—and sometimes more importantly—how they don't answer your probing questions. Find franchisees who have exited the system and get their take. It's imperative to get input from other channels, not just "approved" franchisees and contacts from the franchisor. That will not get you the unvarnished truth. Still, other franchisees may hide the bad aspects from you as they are also protecting their own assets, so digging deeply is necessary.

One franchisee bought into a system that was attempting to expand way too fast and was not able to support the growth. The leadership was not equipped to support the new franchisees and truly didn't have any idea how to structure its system to help franchisees be profitable. Due to the arrogance of the leadership, which we will discuss further in the next chapter, it quickly blamed the franchisees for any deficiencies, not considering that their system or lack thereof was the problem. This left franchisees fending for themselves in many areas of the business. Other areas were affected by this as well, such as training and the ability to support ongoing operations of franchise locations. The franchisor was trying to catch up to demand they were not set up to provide. Regardless, the franchisor continued to sell new franchise locations, collecting many thousands of dollars in franchise fees and product and supply orders from new and naive franchisees.

What is the financial picture of both the franchisor and franchisee?

It's important to know the financial track record of the franchisor. Is the brand growing? Is it stable? How is the brand spending its money? What is the marketing plan or product roadmap for new products and services? How profitable is the franchisor?

You must understand the financial projections for your potential franchise location so you can set your expectations and plan accordingly. In the FDD, Item 19 is where the franchisor can disclose the earnings claims of existing franchise and corporate locations but this data is not mandatory. Also, any data provided may not represent **all** franchisees and corporate locations. Be sure to read the fine print to fully understand exactly what data is—and isn't—included. It can be easy to make the data look how a franchisor wants, depending on the information included. For example, if only very successful franchise location data is included, the financial projection will be skewed high. Remember there is a tendency for a franchisor to put their best foot forward. By coaching franchisees, I have learned that franchisors have a propensity to blame individual franchisees for lower sales rather than review their own business model to understand how it may be limiting the success of the franchisee.

For good franchisors, the entry for Item 19 can be a thorough and detailed representation of existing franchisees and helpful in your analysis of the franchise system. It's important to see as complete a picture as you can, so asking follow-up questions and reaching out to additional franchisees is crucial before you make a long-term commitment.

Financial results as a franchisee will vary and depend on how you run your business. You may hire a full-time manager or manage the franchise yourself. Either scenario will significantly affect your personal profit potential. Don't let the franchisor gloss over this discussion. Owning this franchise may be your day job for years so you need to understand what you are getting into. Alternatively, if a franchise is pitched as an absentee-owner business, make sure to verify the financials presented and that there are franchises in the system operating as such at a profit. Running an unprofitable business, especially as an absentee owner, is a recipe for disaster.

Another franchisee found that he and other franchisees were expected to cash flow their locations on the liability sales of gift certificates and pre-purchased discounted services. While this was not in writing, after the first holiday gift certificate sale, the franchisor told franchisees, "You did great! Now you can use that money to carry you until Mother's Day gift certificate sales and that will cash-flow you to the next gift certificate sale . . ." and so on. Essentially, this involved promoting the use of liability funds instead of saving at least a portion to fund the expenses incurred in producing the services in the future. This was not discussed during the purchasing phase; if it had been, it would likely have become apparent that financial projections would fall apart. In other words, the franchisor's business model for franchisees would not generate revenue as described in the FDD unless the cash used for all liabilities sales was used in the current year's profitability calculations. The franchisee described it almost like a Ponzi scheme—moving money forward to cover expenses in hopes of never having to redeem the liabilities. And even worse, saddling a franchisee with these liabilities on their books made selling the franchise more difficult for franchisees who wanted to get out. It took many franchisees a few years to fully experience the negative effects of this and then they were stuck feeling they had only bought themselves a job, not a business. Later, they had to figure out some way to offload their franchise; either selling it to other potential franchisee owners (who didn't perform their due diligence!) or selling it back to the franchisor for peanuts.

When the franchisee was attempting to sell and reviewed the opportunity with an attorney, the attorney also referenced the business as being somewhat of a Ponzi scheme. Of course, a "Ponzi-like scheme" was **not** inferred anywhere in the FDD; franchisees only learned this after purchasing the franchise when it was too late.

Lack of financial planning for franchise locations' potential success was also evident early on for another franchisee. All franchisees were invited to a meeting held at the corporate office after several new franchisees were brought on board. The VP of franchise operations holding the meeting was asked by a new franchisee about how much franchisees should expect to earn as a percentage of sales and other metrics so they could all detail their proformas for the upcoming year. The question was very matter-of-fact and diplomatically acknowledged that each location was different as were other factors including size, staff, service offerings, hours of operation, stage of growth, etc. The question was to solicit additional information on how to plan their own business based on the franchisor's 30 years of business operations. The franchisee remembers all the new franchisees were optimistic and truly wanted to lead their locations for success in partnership with the franchisor.

The response from the VP was strange, to say the least. The VP became extremely angry, offered an inadequate and frankly, ignorant response, and within five minutes, the franchisee who asked the question was escorted out of the room by franchise leadership! Every financial question was discouraged and met with anger. There was zero interest in learning the issues franchisees had or understanding franchisee cost structures. The franchisor later turned such questions into ways to berate franchisees for low revenue. However, the franchisor regularly required franchisees to foot the bill for new products and offer discounts more often than the locations could support with little to no notice or explanation for the strategy. This franchisee doesn't remember anyone at the corporate office having any interest in helping them increase their profits.

The financial toll a franchisor can put on franchisees is subjective and random. With little integrity, a franchisor can quickly and fatally put a franchise location in the position of being unable to pay its bills due to the ineptitude or unethical nature of the franchisor. In any event, the franchisee has signed on the dotted line and may have a lease, staff, and customers to serve, so franchisees tend to soldier on amid a fundamentally flawed system. Know what you are getting into.

A good franchisor will want you to know the financial situation so you can be successful, maintain the brand, and help increase profits overall. They will understand the cost structure that the franchisees must operate under, the changing industry, and have a plan for growth so as not to chip away at franchisees' profits. They won't blame franchisees for difficulties—they'll appreciate that the franchisee wants a smooth-running and profitable business. In good situations, both parties feel great.

One franchisee bought into a brand that had been in business for 25 years in a mature industry. However, the fairly new franchisor simply didn't understand how to lead for top-line growth. There was little innovation and competition was leaving the brand in the dust. The franchisor's growth strategy essentially was to sit back and wait until their franchisees were desperate enough to sell back their franchise for almost nothing. Ironically, even then, the now corporate-owned locations weren't thriving, and eventually the franchisor exited the business entirely.

The point of this section is to understand the financial potential for the franchise—both the high end and the low end—**before** you buy it. This information is gleaned from other franchisees in the system, and good franchisors will strive to provide accurate numbers for you.

Ask everyone at the corporate office and all franchisees every financial question to put together a complete financial picture. Understand the numbers so you can make an educated decision. Do not expect the franchisor to provide everything you need and do not be blinded and think you are special and can do better than the numbers you uncover through your diligence. Sales tactics pitting you against other "not so good" franchisees are common and lead to inflated ideas of what you can do. You can be the best business operator ever, but with a bad franchise model that you have no control over, you will never be able to reach the revenue potential you could with a good franchise model.

Use the information provided in Item 19 in combination with what you can gather yourself to see the realistic revenue of the potential franchise location/unit. Talk with other franchisees to learn how long it can take to break even and whether there are generally low- and high-revenue months to help with planning. All of this information is invaluable as you move into unknown territory.

What is the time commitment required for this franchise?

When considering a franchise location, one franchisee-to-be met with the VP of franchise sales and was told that they were seeking business people to buy their franchises and that one could, just like George Foreman with his grill, "set it and forget it" and essentially operate it as an absentee owner. However, in a conversation with the VP of operations after buying, the franchisee was told "We like the owner/operators [to be there full-time to make sure] it's running properly." There was no consistent message from the corporate office as to what their business model was and/or how their franchises were best run. The message was tailored by the VP of sales to tell franchisees what he thought they wanted to hear. Leadership was figuring it out as they went along with differing opinions and plans without the data necessary for decision-making.

The franchisee was determined to do what was necessary and believed he was up for the challenge even though he hadn't signed up for it. He did make it work for a while, but better franchisor systems and plans would have made it a more successful business for him **and** the franchisor. Since then, many locations have closed and the brand has weakened immensely. Franchisees who bought into the system expecting to be absentee owners quickly found out they weren't fully supported by the divided leadership team. And amid unclear systems to support these owners, many quickly exited the system, frustrated and at with large financial losses.

To assess the likely time commitment in a particular system, reach out to existing franchisees. Understand that all franchisees will choose to run their businesses slightly differently, but some penetrating questions to help flesh this out for you include:

- What is the overall time requirement as a franchisee?
- What is your schedule (if appropriate to the franchise) at the location?
- What are the main tasks you perform weekly?
- How much time do you spend at the corporate office?
- What is required/preferred by your franchise agreement regarding time spent or working hours?
- What does the successful franchise model look like for this brand?
- Are there meetings at the corporate office? How many? How much notice is given?

- Are there day-to-day work/revenue requirements or expectations from the franchisor?
- What do you see as weekly requirements and priorities for the franchise?
- Where do you spend your working time each week?
- When did you last take a full week away from your business?
- Do you always need to be available to your employees or the franchisor?
- What was the timeline to get your franchise open?
- What help did corporate leadership provide?
- Are there typical slow times during the year as to time commitment and revenue production?

How is marketing handled and how much is needed/expected for your franchise?

Marketing is handled differently by various franchise systems. Typically, a franchisee will pay into a marketing/advertising fund every month as a percentage of revenue which can be about 2–3% of monthly revenue. Generally, the franchisor can spend this fund as they choose. It's important to understand how this money has been spent in the past and when, what geographic areas it targets, what products and services it offers promotions on, etc., to know how it may influence sales for your location. You'll want to capitalize on this promotional activity with your own advertising and get your staff up to speed on whatever promotion in your location is applicable. Talk with other franchisees to learn how you should budget for marketing and your grand opening as well.

One franchisee reported that their franchise system did the majority of its advertising around a few major promotions, including a lot of digital ads and social media marketing around major holidays. However, the ads didn't cover the territory of some of the more remotely located franchises and they were not granted advertising funds to support them. Before signing the FDD, negotiate marketing funds to support your location as equitably as other locations since you'll be paying into the fund.

About a year into their franchise ownership, a franchisee learned that his corporate office gave away a lot of gift certificates to purchase a large part of holiday advertising. Some told him that they were paid for with gift certificates that could be redeemed at any location, even independent franchise locations and he received many of these gift certificates early on. Later, some of the gift certificates were labeled discreetly as only valid at corporate-owned franchise locations, but the VP of operations told him "It's just good business to redeem them anyway," which would mean the franchisee would get zero for performing a $100+ services per customer and still have to pay his staff for providing these products—purchased from the franchisor—to customers. This was quite disconcerting.

In a booming economy and high-growth business, this can be dealt with from time to time, but he had a few Saturdays (prime days for business) filled up with these free services. He was not told about this ahead of time and paid his royalties each month; a percentage of which was supposed to go to marketing costs, but then he would have to redeem free services so his franchisor didn't have to fork out the cash for advertising. This franchisee felt it was a farce and having to fight to get reimbursed for these gift certificates after being nickel and dimed repeatedly was exhausting. Owning and running a business is tough enough without having to squabble with the very people you were **paying** to support you and help to grow the brand. They did not have the franchisee's best interest in mind and got free advertising on the backs of their franchisees.

Looking at his franchise documents, one could find vague references to promos but would not think it would be on a regular basis. This systematically screwed the franchisees while telling them it was "good for business."

What areas will I be responsible for and have control over?

To effectively open your franchise, there will likely be some systems, services, and/or processes over which you will have independent control. For example, accounting, insurance, payroll, and utilities are things you will likely have to set up. It's important to learn this ahead of time so you can be selective in choosing vendors. Reaching out to other franchisees in the system to get vendor information can be invaluable, as working with vendors who already know the franchise system can be time- and cost-effective. Again, each franchise system operates differently, and learning this can help you know if a particular franchise system would work for you. Talking with other independent franchise owners helped me to find quality and cost-effective insurance and payroll processing providers, among others.

One franchisee was provided with a set-cost system that included POS and inventory purchasing. Equipment and product purchases from the franchisor are also regularly required by the franchisee.

Is there a support system available besides the franchisor?

One franchisee found that her franchisor frowned upon the franchisees meeting together without a representative from the corporate office. The franchisees had set up a monthly meeting to discuss ways to support each other, as they all were working in the same industry and the same businesses. However, the franchisor used bully tactics to make it known that the meetings were not appreciated and some franchisees stopped meeting out of fear.

Other franchise systems have authorized groups and meet often, similar to a union. Had there been an official group, the franchisee believes that they could have had a much better business ownership experience and even helped the franchisor. The franchisor would have become more knowledgeable of franchisee issues instead of deciding that the franchisees didn't know what they were doing. Up to her last day with her franchise, the franchisor said things that didn't make any sense, showing how out of touch they were with the franchise locations; the franchisees' insights would have been beneficial for the franchisor.

Finding meetups, small business groups in the same industry, or a business coach, among other areas of support, can be great. Set these up before opening because once your franchise is open, you will be extremely busy but will need support more than ever.

CHAPTER 6

DO YOU WANT TO BE IN BUSINESS WITH THE LEADERSHIP OF THE FRANCHISE?

Franchise brands are companies. Companies are run by people. Therefore, franchise brands are run by people. In many cases, companies that franchise their business have been created by one person or few people who initially created a brand, opened a location or two, and decided to franchise it based on the success they had. In other cases, a person may purchase a franchise company and become the franchisor of an existing brand. Others still are purchased by private equity businesses that effectively put people in charge of running the franchise. So it all comes back to people.

In every case, **people** are leading the franchise brand company. The person in charge of the operation has much control over franchisees. Just as in a regular business, whoever is in charge can make it the best work experience their employees ever had—or can make life a living hell. However, franchisees cannot just quit. They own a franchise. If your franchisor is not up to the challenge or is an unethical franchisor, unfortunately, it can be a losing proposition for you before you even become operational.

This chapter strongly encourages you to evaluate the **people** who will have much control over your success as a franchisee in their system. Examine this evaluation in two distinct areas:

- Is leadership capable?
- Is leadership ethical?

Being capable speaks to the leadership's ability to create and maintain brand value. Is the leadership capable of growing the brand's bottom line? Meaning, does the leadership have a strategy for growth with products and/or services? Does the leadership have a plan for franchise growth that grows the overall brand so franchisee locations and the franchisor both profit? Is there a long-term plan for growth and a financial plan to support it? And if the leadership lacks in any of these areas, do they find others to help fill the gaps? Is the leadership open-minded and coachable in areas that need improvement to reach the full potential of the brand?

In other words, *is the franchisor a great leader?* Everyone needs help in some areas of a business; leadership can't know everything all the time. But a great franchisor must recognize what they lack, reach out to others, hire well, etc., to create a great brand and continue learning as they lead a franchise. Do not underestimate this. I've coached franchisees who have experienced a franchisor who lacked these qualities. The skills required to start and run a single location of a successful business are very different from the skills needed to be a franchisor and lead tens or hundreds of franchisees to scale successfully. A leader of a franchise needs to be capable of leading the brand for this type of growth and engaging other leaders to do it together.

The second, critical question is whether leadership is ethical. You may have worked with a boss who backstabs employees, pits employees against each other, or flat-out lies. Imagine if this person was your franchisor. As an employee, you may put up with this toxic environment for a while until you find a new job, but as a franchisee, you must work with this toxic "boss" to find a way to end the franchise agreement you signed with them. The franchisor holds a lot of power over how and when you can exit a franchise, so it will be doubly hard to exit if the franchisor is unethical.

Franchisees are a source of revenue for the franchisor. In good franchise systems, the franchisor's main source of revenue is the royalties that each franchise pays to the franchisor. This makes sense since the franchisor has created and promised to support the brand, provides systems and processes for each franchisee to follow to maintain a great brand, and everyone benefits. However, unethical franchisors will look for ways to squeeze franchisees for more revenue, especially when times are tough. This erodes the brand as franchisees struggle to earn profits; the franchisor is working to grow their revenue mostly on the backs of the franchisees instead of focusing on growing brand revenue for all. This creates a vicious cycle whereby franchises lose profit each year at the hands of additional costs, fees, required upgrades, systems, and products that are required to be purchased from the franchisor—improving revenue and profits for the franchisor only.

In the worst of circumstances, a franchisor is both incapable and unethical. This is a recipe for disaster for franchisees so it is vital to evaluate the competence of the leadership and try to judge whether they are ethical. Past behavior can be an indication and may be gleaned from how a franchisor has dealt with difficult situations previously. Conversing with those who have been in business relationships with the franchisor can be helpful. Researching public legal documents in the courts can also be educational. Listening to how the franchisor's direct reports talk about the franchisor can also be eye-opening. Spend as much time at the franchisor's corporate office as you can **before** purchasing a franchise. Observe how the staff interacts with the franchisor. Get yourself in front of the franchisor often to listen, observe their body language, and learn about them before you buy.

One former franchisee says there were major red flags he did not note when considering his franchise. If you don't feel like the franchisor is generally going to do the right thing when the chips are down, **run**! Owning a business is hard, and being a successful franchisor requires ethical leadership. It can be too tempting for franchisors without a moral compass to turn to the very people they promised to support—the franchisees—to make up for losses on their balance sheet. When this happens year after year, the result is a franchise system that is not growing. In the worst cases, the franchisor's growth strategy becomes waiting for their franchisees to be unable to sell their worthless franchise location to anyone else and taking it over by requiring exorbitant fees to exit the franchise agreement to avoid being sued by the franchisor for breach of contract. This has happened.

Another franchisee shared she spent six months doing tons of work to get ready to open her location—including finding a contractor to design and build out the space, recruiting staff, and buying furniture and fixtures. She was excited to be putting the final touches on her franchise location. When she was about two weeks from opening day and had just finished a day of training at a local, corporate-owned franchise location, she met with the director of franchise operations to discuss her training and next steps. In hindsight, she recalls these meetings had almost always involved the director getting annoyed or even angry by questions the franchisee had for her. As a newbie to the industry, which this franchisor wanted, this is a major red flag and the franchisee now knows she should have run then. The franchise system leadership didn't know how to answer her questions, often hid information, reacted angrily when questioned, and created fear of the repercussions that franchisees would later have to endure. This went on and on. The franchisee discussed this with numerous other franchisees in the system; they had experienced the same treatment many times as well.

One day, a franchisee and the VP of sales discussed his initial order of products—required to be purchased from the franchisor—for resale and used in the process of operations at his franchise. This was a huge order and a significant expense, as you can imagine, as it would stock the entire business for opening and sometime after. Earlier that day, the franchisee had learned from another location manager that the product line was going to be discontinued very soon, so he asked the director of franchise operations about the order. Since the product was going to be discontinued, the franchisee was concerned about purchasing an entirely new line of products shortly after opening. The VP was livid, stating that the franchisee should not have been told about it and that he shouldn't question her.

The franchisee remembers thinking *WTF is going on here?* as he left, feeling attacked for asking a question. He was very grateful to have been told so that he didn't waste too much purchasing a discontinued product line. It was deceitful for the franchisor to hide details that incurred unnecessary costs so they could offload products likely never to sell. When the franchisee was most vulnerable, the franchisor he had just signed on to work with immediately took advantage of his inexperience and ripped him off; he hadn't even opened his doors and was already being treated unethically! He learned very early on that this franchisor could not be trusted. He said leadership seemed to relish the fact that they were "putting one over" on him and other new franchisees until they figured it out.

This is just one example of the fear franchisors would instill in their franchisees and the lack of interest shown in their success. The franchisee was still under the delusion that they wanted him to be set up for success, that his success as a franchisee would mean their success as a franchise system. As time went on it, became clear that the franchisor was waiting to buy the franchisees back for, in their own words, "pennies on the dollar." After that product line blowup, the approach continued for years, with verbal attacks and feedback that one shouldn't ask questions without expecting to get treated like the enemy.

This example, and many, many others will not be found in any franchise documents. A franchisor has much leeway in randomly affecting a franchisee's pocketbook, as this franchisor did time after time.

As discussed earlier, many franchise systems are borne out of one or a few successful locations of a brand with established leadership staff—who become the leaders of the entire franchise system. These people have formed a company culture, and just as in any company, this culture can be toxic and can take a while for a newcomer to recognize it. And again, employees can quit, but the exit steps are much different, more complicated, and can be quite expensive for a franchisee. Take the time to learn who exactly you are getting into business with **before** you sign on the dotted line. It would not have been apparent to frequent customers that the franchisor had a toxic culture.

It is of utmost importance, not just to get a look under the hood of the franchise agreement and other documents, but also to know **who** you are going into business with. Of course, people in leadership may change over the years, but it can still be indicative of future culture, practices, and your ability to succeed within their system.

Normal due diligence will mean you've made the official calls and met with people within the system to understand the franchise system. Other franchisees tell you about day-to-day business and financials, what you can hope to achieve in your business, and the other things that we covered in the last chapter. But this chapter encourages you to examine whether you really want to be in business with the **people** of the franchise system. The franchise agreement can only cover so many things. Finding out how other franchisees are doing can only cover so much. The franchise ecosystem can be a fairly closed system where the franchisor and existing franchisees may want to protect the system; it's their investment, business, and livelihood, so they might conspire intentionally or unintentionally to provide only positive information. You, however, haven't jumped on board just yet and really need to know how they're going to act when things are bad. What has been their past modus operandi when issues have arisen? Have you reached out to franchisees who have left the system? Can you talk to vendors who work with them? Again, no one is perfect, but having an idea of the ethics, practices, and capabilities of the people you will be in business with—and essentially are beholden to—is critical. Many are too naive at the time of purchase.

One franchisee noted her franchisor sitting unusually close to her in a franchise group meeting with many franchisees. This franchisee had recently given birth to a baby and was shocked when the franchisor publicly asked, in a very derogatory way, "How many more kids are you going to have?" The franchisee knew that the franchisor and the VP of operations had spoken to others about how her having children was not a good thing for a franchise owner. And the franchisor chose to make a public statement and send a message to all of the other franchisees.

Again, that threatening and bullying mentality can persist unchecked. This franchisee had taken necessary measures to cover the needs of her franchise business, was in daily contact with the location, and was present at her franchise at a reduced level for six weeks after giving birth.

The franchise "system" didn't work and they were blaming it on the fact that she had recently had a baby as to why sales were not where they felt they should be. She was not an employee and so couldn't just go to HR and report the harassment. She would have had to sue while keeping her business running so as not to default on any franchise agreement rules.

Other franchisees in the system are not likely to tell you any of this and customers are often kept in the dark; as the lifeblood of the franchisees and company, they are shown only the best side of everyone.

Another toxic practice that I've seen in my work with franchisees-to-be, is where a franchisor will say other franchise locations are not doing well because the specific franchisee is not capable. While this can certainly be true, if you hear this repeatedly used as an excuse, you are likely dealing with a franchise system that causes the lack of success. In one case, a franchisor had opened just one location of the brand and proceeded to badmouth the franchisee to the point of telling potential franchisees not to speak to them about insight into the brand. This is a major red flag, but potential franchisees buy it. As a potential franchisee, you may think you'd be different, you'd be better than that "bad" franchisee—the franchisor may even tell you that. But even a great franchisee will not be able to overcome a bad franchise system for any length of time.

I believe most franchisees seek out franchising to work hard and achieve financial success. Franchisees are required to invest large sums of money and are generally looking to get a return on their investment. I am skeptical that all franchisors are working to help their franchisees succeed, especially when a franchisor or franchise system is struggling. A franchisor may blame franchisees as a whole and squeeze them for additional funds through promotions, equipment purchases, and other fees. A captive group of franchisees is an easier pool of potential revenue for a franchisor than actually building the franchise system and brand for growth in the first place, as the leadership of a company should. The franchisee–franchisor relationship is a unique business arrangement, and when in the hands of unethical and/or inept leaders, it is disastrous.

A franchisee was a customer of a particular brand for 8 years before he purchased a franchise. He was not aware of problems when he visited different franchise and corporate locations; the people working there were very professional, as it was their livelihood. It was not until he got close enough to the business as a franchisee that negative issues became obvious almost immediately.

However, if you are like him, you are fairly invested in the franchise purchase working out and may disregard negative information. You may feel you can be a "better" franchisee than those the franchisor is putting down and continue into franchise ownership. Don't be fooled. If something seems strange from the start, run away quickly.

Go to local courthouses to find any public records of litigation against a potential franchisor brand or the franchisor personally. You may find a large number of cases or that a franchisor is quite litigious. Had franchisees known this ahead of time, I don't believe that they would have bought into the franchise system. Don't take what is reported in the FDD as all the facts. Do your own research;

you may not learn this information from your franchise attorney. Remember, the franchisor is putting their best foot forward to make a large sale. You must uncover the truth. No one will be as vested in the truth more than you.

I don't mean to paint every franchise system in a bad light here but I know many franchise systems have major issues and want you to take the time to really investigate the franchise you are considering. Search for any skeletons and pitfalls that may befall you along the way.

Of course, when things are going well, sales are good, and the entire franchise system is growing, you may run into fewer problems. However, when there are problems and sales are not increasing, your franchisor—in an ideal world— will be figuring out ways to grow the overall business and bring more customers to the franchises. This strategy would increase everyone's growth. But this may not be the case for all franchisors.

The overall industry of one franchise system was becoming more competitive and the franchisor didn't know what to do. Leadership tried adding some different services to no avail, then nickeled and dimed franchisees to a point unsustainable for the franchisees; the franchise had no interest in listening to the franchisees' feedback for growth. These things didn't come to light in reviewing franchise documents or few would have bought into this franchise system.

Some report that the depth of promotions franchisees were required to take part in was also not included in the FDD. I don't think anybody even guessed that drastic reductions in the prices of services and products would be required, significantly cutting into profit.

If it occurs for several years and diminishes the value of franchise locations, it essentially deems them unsellable at market price. This reduces the potential of any franchise ever reselling and keeps a potential buyer in the dark.

Reach out to franchisees that have exited the system. These can be hard to find because there may be an NDA or other agreement barring them from talking about their exit details. If you are unable to reach franchisees that have exited after a few attempts, or who won't give you a statement or a moment of their time, I would consider that a red flag. And I suggest you explore it further until you get answers, but know some people just don't fit a particular franchise.

One franchisee chuckled to herself when remembering her first holiday season as a new franchisee. She had been open for about six months and was sending holiday cards. She wrote to the franchisor and a couple of people at the top who helped open her business saying she was so happy to be in business together and looked forward to growing the company with them. She thought that they were truly in business **together**. When she later saw them in person, they almost looked at her like she was nuts; there was no working "together" on this. She had been treated badly by the franchisor and would continue to be, but when a small morsel of focus was extended to her and others, the franchisees were ingratiated.

It's important to know how someone acts when their back is against the wall. How did the franchisor react under tough circumstances? Did they help and support the franchisees or throw them under the bus?

One franchisor made a concerted effort to keep franchisees apart from each other in a sort of "divide and conquer" style so they wouldn't know anything about the other franchisees. Leadership would stir up competition between them inciting fear, distrust, and belief that the others were bad business people. This was done with almost all of the franchisees in the franchise system.

One specific example was when franchisees got together as a group once a month to review expenses. For the most part, they reviewed outside costs and promotional plans for particular locations. The franchisor got wind of these meetings, was uncomfortable with the idea, and began trying to end them. When the group came up with a few requests for corporate, they were met with threats. Some individual franchisees stopped attending the meetings, afraid it would hurt their relationship with the corporate office.

I am aware of similar issues in other franchise systems and invite you to research online each specific franchise system you are evaluating. I wouldn't take any published lists of best franchises at face value. Research how these rankings are determined.

It's not automatically obvious to some franchisors that growing a franchise system grows franchisees as well, and working symbiotically is expected. Excited and gullible franchisees-to-be may not believe that a franchisor could turn out to be their enemy and as inept and unethical as some report. Of course, not all franchisors are bad. But if you do become chained to one, it can quickly become hell. The purpose of this book is to keep that from happening to you.

DISENFRANCHISED

CHAPTER 7

IS THERE AN ACCEPTABLE PATH TO EXITING THE FRANCHISE?

F iling for personal bankruptcy or getting sued by your franchisor are things you do not think of when you are excited about franchise ownership. However, knowing the best paths to exiting your franchise ownership is critical. It's not fun to think about, but you must understand what the FDD contains and how the process of ending your franchise agreement is outlined by your franchisor. If after owning your franchise for a while there are issues with the franchise system, the brand is declining, or other problems, you may not find a buyer to pay what you need—if you can find one at all. If this is the case, you will need your franchisor's assistance and approval, and under these difficult circumstances, a franchisor may not be the most helpful. It can be painful and not what you would wish on anyone.

One franchisor offered little to no help over the two years a franchisee worked with a business broker, talked with other franchisees within the system, and tried to figure out how to sell the "investment" to someone else. The franchisor sat by silently. As the end of the franchise agreement approached and knowing only a fool would renew it, the franchisor bought the franchise for almost nothing after tacking on unnecessary fees.

If people leading the franchise system practice unethically, a franchisee is put in a no-win situation when a franchise agreement does not lay out a process to exit the franchise reasonably. Franchisees are viewed as a revenue stream right up to the end of the relationship with no regard for the work put in growing the brand. Don't get caught up in the excitement at the beginning of your due diligence process and neglect to plan for the exit. You will need to exit your franchise eventually; knowing the rules from the start will allow you to enjoy your business ownership more and thoughtfully determine when and how to plan your exit.

Many franchisees purchase a franchise with their hard-earned money, wanting to realize the dream of owning and growing a business with a brand for mutual benefit. Some franchisors are not interested in supporting franchisees to exit their system and will make efforts otherwise.

When things go south for a franchise brand, it may get to a point where only a potential buyer completely in the dark would buy the franchise, and the franchisor knows this. When this happens, some franchisors sit back and wait while the franchisee flounders so they can take over the franchise location and make it a corporate location, often at a cost to the franchisee. Granted, if the franchisor's business model was meant to work, buyers would be interested in buying and growing franchises. If the franchisor is not capable or interested in that, the system fails before one even attempts to sell.

Some former franchisees have had to file bankruptcy, were shut down and sued by their franchisor, or continued to work in indentured servitude, to the decline of their mental and physical health.

Franchisors may even use their franchisees' experiences and create a sense of fear so current franchisees are deterred from any action to sever the contract. Again, the power structure of the franchisee–franchisor relationship is unbalanced and puts the franchisee at a disadvantage. Lying, trumped-up charges, and false accusations toward franchisees have occurred during these difficult times, taking advantage of the franchisee at extremely vulnerable times in the business ownership.

I've also known the leadership of franchise systems to successfully transfer a location to others or wind down a location if the model or location was no longer working, so experiences vary. It's imperative to know how your potential franchisor will handle exiting their system. You must understand what is written in the FDD about exiting your business and have clearly documented what the outcome can be in the event of a failing system. As I said earlier, it is important to learn what others have experienced in the franchise system you are considering.

The following points need to be considered and understood regarding ending any particular franchise agreement:

- What is written in a franchise agreement can be implemented differently by different people under different circumstances, so it is important for the agreement to clearly state the steps to exit.
- Can you close down if you've taken adequate time to try to sell?
- What are the rules and ramifications if you shut down your franchise location?
- Can you transfer ownership to someone else?
- Does the franchisor have to approve the new franchisee and if so, under what conditions?
- What fees and royalties still need to be paid on lost revenue if you just walk away from your franchise?

Details about how to get out of a franchise may not be fully articulated in the FDD, so it largely comes down to the relationship. As a new franchisor—once the FDD is completed—one may not consider the protection necessary for both parties and what is required when a franchisee is exiting.

Some franchisors take advantage of the franchisees. You may feel that franchisees-to-be should have clearly understood the franchise agreement's exit requirements and planned their exit accordingly much sooner. It may seem unfathomable to you that a franchisor would choose to prey on their franchisees in this manner, especially after franchisees work so hard for years to help grow the brand. But this can be the reality. Other franchise systems allow a location to close with the franchisor's approval or, better yet, set up portals where franchisees can list their location for sale to both other franchisees and outside buyers.

There is a tendency to not be too concerned with how to sell or close down a franchise when getting started. But it is imperative to understand the details in your agreement to formulate your exit strategy. While it may be exciting to think of leaving your business to a younger family member, the likelihood of that happening is very slim. Some agreements state that if one closes, they would have to pay royalties based on historical sales data, in effect having to pay monthly royalties even if they're unable to operate the business and the brand is declining. Unfortunately, I know of franchisors who enforce this.

Think of the exit plan almost like a prenuptial agreement. Just as no one wants to think about the new partnership ending, you will likely not want to spend too much time thinking that the franchisee–franchisor arrangement might end badly. However, it is vital to know how it will go because it is more likely than a marriage to eventually end. Having a clear plan laid out while you are on speaking terms and being "sold to" will get you the most advantageous results.

CHAPTER 8

NEXT STEPS

If you've read this far in the book and can answer an emphatic YES to each of these four important questions . . .

1. YES, you are a good fit to be a franchisee.
2. YES, you have determined that the franchise system is worth your investment.
3. YES, you would like to be in business with the management of the franchise system.
4. YES, there is an acceptable path to exiting the franchise.

. . . then you may choose to proceed cautiously to purchase the franchise you have evaluated.

If you want to be a franchisee but haven't found the right opportunity, keep looking. They are out there but may take some time to find. You are doing the right thing in walking away from a deal that doesn't meet your criteria. When you find the one, you'll be very glad you took the time.

Use this checklist to review each franchise opportunity.

Is this my "perfect" franchise?

- Is the location perfect? Why or why not?
- Have I confirmed with other franchisees that the financials are "as advertised"?
- Have I met with and asked two to four existing franchisees my long list of questions and checked to see if their answers were consistent?
- Have I met with two ex-franchisees?
- Have I spoken with most of the corporate staff? Do I support their past decisions and growth plans? Do they have a long-term growth plan I like and support?
- Have they evaded or not answered any of my questions?
- Have I researched any litigation?
- Am I satisfied that the hours required for the franchise ownership are "as advertised"?
- Have I mapped out a weekly schedule for the first few months of what will be required of me to own/operate the franchise, and does it work for me?
- Are there systems in place by the franchisor for payroll? Marketing? Advertising? Training? Accounting? Vendors needed? Cleaning services? Maintenance services? All supplies? All equipment?

- If it is a new location, is there support ready to help open the location? Do I know what I will need to acquire on my own?
- If it is an existing location, will there be a transition period/ schedule with the current owner? What will I need to establish to take over the location? Payroll? Staff changes?
- Have I assured (in writing) that my location will be part of the corporate advertising?
- Have I been assured (in writing) that my territory is protected?
- Have I reviewed the FDD with an attorney and other franchisees?

Something else to also consider: Is the franchisor new to franchising? I've known some who got into a franchise system early and it was great as the franchisors were anxious for success (not jaded from the pain of being a franchisor) and territories weren't crowded. On the other hand, if no one has heard of the brand, it can be a good thing or a bad thing. Also, is the brand oversaturated? Even a great brand can be a horrible experience for its franchisees if management is terrible. Signing on with a franchise that isn't great can quickly make your life a living hell. **Do not rush into a mediocre franchise system.** Please trust me on this.

If you have answered **no** to being a good franchisee candidate, you have probably just avoided much agony and dodged a bullet. You may have helped yourself avoid a terrible situation with some self-reflection and can now move toward something that is a better fit for your success.

Some areas to consider as you determine your next steps:

- What sparked your interest in a franchisee? Was it a particular industry? If so,
  - Explore roles in the industry or work at a franchise or other small business in that industry
  - Look for industry groups and organizations to join
  - Find people in roles you want and reach out to them
- Was it the lure of owning your own business? If so,
  - Is there a business you can start on your own—even as a side hustle—to get more involved before leaping?
  - Seek out roles working for another small business in your field of interest
  - Join small business groups in person or online to find your next stop
  - If you have both the industry and desire to own a small business in mind, consider starting your own business in that field
  - Volunteer in the industry of interest
  - Become an independent contractor in the industry
  - Reach out to several people connected with the industry and meet with each for exploratory discussions
  - If you think you'd like to buy a franchise in the future, get a job at a franchise location; low risk, high learning opportunity

Chapter 9

FINAL THOUGHTS

As a former franchisee and one who coaches current and former franchisees, I've listed some of the most important things I have learned.

- Understand that as a franchisee, you are not in control of the brand. You are obligated to follow the franchisor's rules.
- Consider bowing out early if you learn the franchise model, industry, brand, etc., is just not working. It can be self-destructive and detrimental to your mental and financial health to try to work against a franchise system. It is not quitting; it is planning how to get out of a bad deal.
- Staffing and managing people is hard.
- Set clear boundaries for what will work and what won't.
- Find support outside of the franchise system—whether a paid coach or honest, dependable friend—for perspective early and often throughout what can be a roller coaster of a ride as a franchisee.

- Owning a business is gratifying.
- Be cautiously optimistic. Hope and work for the best, but also plan for the worst-case scenario.
- Take plenty of time to validate that a franchise is a good one (hence, this book). Being a customer of a brand is very different from being a franchise owner of that same brand.

I wish you all the best in your quest to find a perfect franchise or your next opportunity. I hope this book has opened your eyes a bit to the reality of franchise ownership, and that you will take your time making a choice, and have a plan for yourself throughout your franchise ownership. Some franchisees feel trapped in a "job" they can't get out of without a lot of pain, but other brand franchisees wouldn't trade their business for another career. Aligning with a brand at the right time that has good management and a growth plan can be a great career path.

FRANCHISING TERMS TO KNOW

Advertising Fee: Fee franchisees pay to the franchisor for their share of the overall advertising spend for the franchise system.

Advertising Fund: The pool of money used by the franchisor to fund marketing efforts for the franchise brand. Generally, all franchisees are required to contribute to this fund regularly, typically monthly.

Approved Site: Physical location of a franchise that is suitable and acceptable to the franchisor.

Area Developer: Some franchise systems use area developers to sell franchises within a specific geographic location over time.

Area Franchisee: A franchisee who has purchased exclusive rights to build franchises in a defined geographical area and who typically is under a timeline for opening them as required by the agreement signed with the franchisor.

Area Representative: In some franchise systems, a franchisee may also be a sales representative of the franchisor in a specified area. Area representatives may receive a commission for bringing new franchisees to the franchisor.

Assets: Resources with economic value that an individual owns with the expectation that it will provide a future benefit or be used to pay a debt.

Break-even: The point at which a business (franchise location) earns enough revenue to cover investment costs.

Business Plan: A franchisee-provided written document detailing overall goals and specific plans and budgets for the franchise.

Candidate: A prospective franchisee who has reached out to a franchisor to potentially purchase one or more franchise locations.

Capital: Available wealth in money or assets owned by a franchisee to purchase a franchise, other business, or investment.

Churning: Turning over franchise ownership from one franchisee to another, the termination and closing of a franchise, or turning a franchisee location into a company-owned location.

Collateral: Resources, belongings, or something of value pledged for repayment of a loan that is surrendered if default on the loan occurs.

Company-Owned Location/Corporate Location: A location owned and operated by the corporate entity of the brand, not an independently operated franchise location that is owned by a franchisee. Also referred to as corporate units.

Conversion: Changing an existing business into a franchise. Some franchisors prefer to convert existing businesses into franchise locations as it reduces costs and risk since the new franchise owner was running a successful business before the conversion and is a proven quantity.

Copyright: Protects an item from being used without permission and gives exclusive right to use and/or license to others to use.

Discovery Day: A show-and-tell or meet-and-greet day typically at a franchisor's corporate offices. Prospective franchisees can learn more about the franchisor and franchise system. This usually includes meeting company leadership and possibly other franchisees and/or prospective franchisees.

Earnings Claim: Actual or forecasted franchise sales, earnings, or profits stated by the franchisor in Item 19 of the Franchise Disclosure Document (FDD).

Equity: Worth or value of an asset minus what is owed on it through a mortgage or loan.

Feasibility Study: Determines whether a person or geographic area is equipped or capable to support a business location such as a franchise.

Federal Trade Commission (FTC): United States government agency that promotes consumer protection laws and antitrust. The FTC aims to eliminate and prevent anti-competitive business practices within the franchise industry.

Field Consultant: Consultants some franchisors hire to support franchisees in their locations; they are typically assigned to support specific geographic areas.

Franchise: Entity or person contracted with a franchisor authorizing the operation and distribution of goods and/or services using the franchisor's brand and franchise system for a fee.

Franchise Agreement (FA): Contract between the franchisee and the franchisor. A signed FA allows the franchisee to open a franchise. Details in the FA include ownership term (typically five to twenty years in duration).

Franchise Attorney: A lawyer who specializes in franchise law.

Franchise Broker: A person or business, typically working with multiple franchisors, hired by a franchisor to find potential new franchisees.

Franchise Consultant: A person or business with expertise in the general franchising industry who advises potential buyers exploring a franchise.

Franchise Disclosure Document (FDD): Documentation provided by the Franchisor that details the franchise history, systems, fees, procedures, rules, turnover rates, and other details of the franchise system. The FDD was previously called a Uniform Franchise Offering Circular (UFOC).

Franchise Expo: Event where prospective franchisees can meet with many franchisors, usually in-person, to evaluate opportunities franchisors offer.

Franchise Fee: Part of the initial investment costs incurred by a franchisee, it is a one-time fee paid to a franchisor that grants a franchisee use of the franchise's brand and likeness.

Franchise Operations: All of the procedures, strategies, and processes required by franchise businesses to provide products and services to a franchise's customers.

Franchise Satisfaction Index (FSI): Created by the Franchise Business Review, it is a 100-point scale measuring the satisfaction of franchise owners of a brand.

Franchise System: Owned by a franchisor, it is the overall administration of a company offering and awarding franchises.

Franchise Unit: An individual location or chapter of the franchise that can be company-owned or franchised.

Franchisee: An individual (or partnership or corporation) who purchases the right to operate a business from a franchisor using the franchisor's brand name and operates using the franchisor's systems.

Franchisor: A person or company granting a franchisee the right to operate a business under the franchisor's trade name using the methods and systems of the franchisor.

Initial (Franchise) Investment/Start-up Costs: An estimate of the total investment a franchisee needs to start a franchise location. It is usually shown in a range, with a high-end and a low-end for each investment category. The initial investment or initial franchise investment is found in Item 7 of the FDD. Investment cost categories include the franchise fee, lease costs, equipment, and product costs, among other start-up costs.

International Franchise Association (IFA): The largest and best-known organization representing the franchising industry. It provides resources to franchisors, franchisees, and suppliers.

Item 19: A section of the FDD where a franchisor discloses earnings claims of existing franchise and corporate locations. Inclusion of this data is not mandatory and may not represent all franchisees and corporate locations. The fine print should state what data is included and what is not.

Lender: Financial institution or bank that provides business loans for franchisees.

License/Licensing: Legal rights to a protected property for a fee.

Liquid Capital: Assets that can easily be converted to cash. Generally, franchisors require franchisees to have a set amount of minimum liquid capital available.

Low-Cost Franchise: A franchise with a low initial investment, typically under $100,000.

Marketing: Planning, promoting, pricing, selling, and distributing services and products to gain customers and satisfy business needs.

Master Franchise: An agreement between a franchisor and a franchisee allowing the franchisee to sell multiple franchises in a specified geographic region. The Master Franchisee may or may not own franchises in the specified geographic region.

Multi-Concept Franchisee: A franchisee who owns more than one franchise unit of different franchise brands.

Multi-Unit Franchisee: A franchisee who owns more than one franchise unit of a brand typically within a defined territory.

Net Worth: Total value of assets after subtracting liabilities. Franchisors may require prospective franchisees to meet a minimum net worth figure.

Operations Manual: A document produced by the franchisor that contains instructions for a franchisee on how to operate the franchise.

Personal Guarantee: A promise in writing to personally guarantee payment on a loan or other business debt if the business does not pay it.

Pro Forma: Financial statements completed using historical data to predict the future.

Renewal: The extension of an originally executed franchise agreement where a franchisee continues ownership of the franchise for a new term.

Return on Investment (ROI): The percentage of the current value of a business relative to the cost of starting it, calculated as: (current value: total cost to start business) / total cost * 100. For example, a business that cost $250,000 to start and is now worth $500,000 has an ROI of 100% ($500,000: $250,000) / $250,000 * 100.

Royalties (or Royalty Fee): Fees paid to a franchisor to remain a franchisee, typically paid monthly as a percentage of the overall revenue of each franchise.

Run rate: Based on past revenue, it can predict future revenue assuming the same level of business.

Supplier/Vendor: A person business providing a product or service to a business. Many franchisors use preferred vendors and suppliers who provide franchisees products and services at established pricing, often at a discount.

Term of Agreement: The length of time the franchisee and franchisor have agreed to partner as such.

Territory: The specific area included in the franchise service geographic area. Franchisors often sell exclusive territories to franchisees to prevent conflicts among franchisees.

Trademark: Identification legally associated with a franchise brand, such as a brand name or logo. It is protected by law and denoted with the symbol ™. Official franchisees are generally permitted to use a franchise's trademarked name and logo.

Transfer: To move ownership of a franchise business from one person or company to another.

Turnover: When a franchise agreement is terminated, transferred, not renewed, or goes out of business.

Uniform Franchise Offering Circular (UFOC): The original name of the Franchise Disclosure Document (FDD).

Validation: Due diligence prospective franchisees should perform before buying a franchise. It includes speaking with existing franchisees to confirm the opportunity as described by the franchisor. The franchisor typically provides a list of franchisees to contact, but prospective franchisees should contact many more than the approved list, including exited franchisees and vendors, suppliers, and additional employees of the corporate office.

Working Capital: Money needed to operate a franchise before it becomes profitable, including the lease, advertising, insurance, salaries, and legal costs.

ABOUT THE AUTHOR

Kara Chmielewski is a small business mentor, angel investor, program management professional, and former franchise owner. Kara has a BS in Electrical Engineering from Worcester Polytechnic Institute and an MBA from Babson College. Kara lives in the Greater Boston area with her husband and three adult children.

www.ingramcontent.com/pod-product-compliance
Lightning Source LLC
Chambersburg PA
CBHW040929210326
41597CB00030B/5241